Most Haunted THEATRES

First published in 2024 by
Andersen Press Limited
20 Vauxhall Bridge Road, London SW1V 2SA, UK
Vijverlaan 48, 3062 HL Rotterdam, Nederland
www.andersenpress.co.uk

2 4 6 8 10 9 7 5 3 1

British Library Cataloguing in Publication Data available.

ISBN 978 1 83913 323 7

Printed and bound in Great Britain by Clays Ltd, Elcograf S.p.A.

Most Haunted THEATRES

YVETTE FIELDING

ILLUSTRATED BY
HANNAH SHAW

ANDERSEN PRESS

THE OLDHAM COLISEUM

THE LYCEUM
THEATRE

THE OLD NICK
THEATRE

TIVOLI VENUE

PAVILION
THEATRE

WINTER GARDENS

THE GAUMONT CINEMA

THEATRE ROYAL

CRAIG Y NOS

INTRODUCTION

Yvette Fielding

Do you believe in ghosts? I do now. I was uncertain what to believe when I was growing up, but I was fascinated and frightened in equal measure. My strange journey into the world of the paranormal began over twenty years ago when my husband Karl and I decided to make a television show about ghosts so we could share our interest with everyone. It was called *Most Haunted* and it changed our lives for ever. Could we spend the night alone in haunted locations with a television camera crew?

After a great deal of thought and a lot of enthusiastic chatter between us and our chosen camera crew, we all excitedly agreed that we could – and were eager to get started as ghost hunters.

It was during the first series of filming *Most Haunted* back in 2002 that we were allowed to spend the night in one of Britain's most famous theatres, the Theatre Royal, Drury Lane, in London.

Armed with a bag of basic ghost-hunting equipment – which consisted of torches, electromagnetic field monitors, pieces of chalk, a stills camera and night-vision cameras – we felt we were ready for anything paranormal that came our way. Over time, as the TV series grew in popularity, so did our ghost-hunting equipment and the bags became heavier and heavier, with all sorts of gadgets and gizmos – you'll learn about all of these later in this book.

It was during this investigation at Drury Lane that I fell in love with the solitude and quietness of empty haunted theatres – but my goodness me, these buildings really come alive at night. It was during this particular investigation that I witnessed my first ghost. It was an experience I'll never forget.

So, what you're about to read are some of my most favourite haunted theatres that I've been lucky enough to investigate with my ghost-hunting team. Perhaps after reading about my spooky adventures, you might decide to go and visit them too.

If you do, keep a watch out, especially for the most famous theatre ghost, the man in grey!

THE THEATRE ROYAL

LOCATION
DRURY LANE, LONDON

GHOSTS
THE MAN IN GREY

CHARLES MACKLIN

JOSEPH GRIMALDI

DAN LENO

PARANORMAL ACTIVITY

ORBS

FLASHES OF COLOURED LIGHT

ELECTRICAL EQUIPMENT TAMPERED WITH

COLD SPOTS

SMELLS OF LAVENDER

SOUNDS OF WHISPERING

FULL GHOSTLY APPARITIONS

BEING TOUCHED AND HIT

POLTERGEIST ACTIVITY

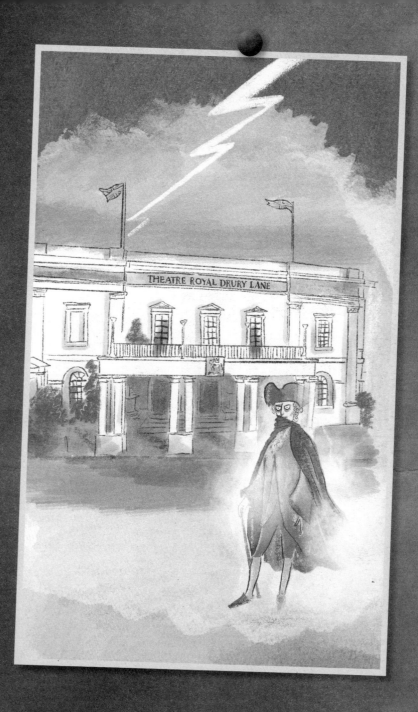

THE HISTORY

Theatre Royal

The Theatre Royal, Drury Lane, is the oldest theatre in London and the original site dates back to the seventeenth century. As you can imagine, its stage has played host to many a famous play and musical throughout the years including *The Lord of the Rings* musical, *Shrek* and *Frozen*. And it's actually the place where 'Rule Britannia' was heard for the very first time by the British public.

The first theatre was built on the site in 1663 by Thomas Killigrew, but it didn't last long as it was consumed by a fire nine years later. The theatre was then rebuilt by the ever-patient Mr Killigrew and remained a popular and successful theatre for nearly 120 years. By then the building needed to be renovated, so its owner at the time, Richard Sheridan, oversaw the demolition of the old theatre and built a new one. Sadly, Mr Sheridan too was to become a victim of fire and, shortly after it was finished, he watched his beloved new theatre go up in flames. Thankfully, a new theatre was designed by Benjamin Dean Wyatt in 1812 and is the building you can still see today. The Theatre Royal has staged thousands of plays and musicals, including *42nd Street* and

Miss Saigon. And making its recent debut there was Disney's *Frozen* production. The theatre is now owned by Andrew Lloyd Webber.

So, who haunts this famous building? Whoever they were, they certainly want to be noticed now! It's the regularity and consistency of the paranormal activity that has been witnessed there so often that makes it such a haunted hotspot and why it is reputed to be the most haunted theatre in the world.

THE HAUNTINGS

THE MAN IN GREY

The ghost of a man in grey is the most famous apparition reported to have been seen at the theatre. It has been spotted many times and quite regularly. The most fascinating sighting was in 1939 when half the cast of a show called *The Dancing Years* were positioned on stage for a photo call. Everyone watched on in amazement and fear as they witnessed a tall ghostly man dressed in grey eighteenth-century clothing, wearing a tricorn hat and a long riding cloak, walk slowly between the rows of seats in the upper circle of the theatre then disappear silently through a wall.

How did all of those people see the same apparition at the same time?

And who was the man in grey? And why does he continue to haunt the theatre?

Some people believe that it could be the ghost of the man whose skeletal remains were discovered in the theatre in the 1800s. During some renovations, builders found that part of a covered wall sounded hollow. They were certain there was a room behind the wall and so, with the theatre's permission, they smashed through the brickwork and plaster to discover a dark secret passageway.

As the builders clambered through all the fallen masonry and into the newly found space, they came across something no one was expecting: a skeleton.

As you can imagine, all the men were totally shocked, as were the staff and owners of the theatre. Weirdly though, the wall the skeleton was found behind is the exact same one that the ghost of the man in grey has been seen disappearing through. The mystery man's bones gave clues to his demise: he was found with his skeletal mouth open wide as if his last breaths were long and torturous. The remaining scraps of clothes he wore were grey and a dagger had been plunged into his ribcage. So, who killed him and why was his body sealed up behind a brick wall?

Some say that the man in grey was an actor at the theatre, possibly Arnold Woodruff, who was allegedly involved in a fight with another man over the love of a woman.

Then who was the other man involved in the fatal fight? Who plunged the dagger? Could it have been another actor? Some say it was the notorious Charles Macklin.

The mystery has never been solved. But I believe the man in grey is Arnold Woodruff and I will never forget the night when *I* saw him, well, part of him, with my own bewildered and terrified eyes. (More on this later.)

CHARLES MACKLIN (1699-1797)

Charles Macklin was an Irish actor and dramatist. He is no longer famous for his talents on stage, the plays he wrote, or the fact that he revolutionised acting techniques. He is best known for the murder of a fellow thespian,

Thomas Hallam. The story goes that the two actors were in the green room of the theatre when a fight broke out over a wig. Charles, in a fit of rage shouted out: 'Goddamn you for a blackguard, scrub, rascal!' and then proceeded to plunge his cane into Thomas's eye – killing him instantly. Amazingly, Charles wasn't found guilty and didn't go to prison. The court declared the case an 'accidental killing'.

A frightening spectre has been seen in the backstage area of the theatre. He's described as a tall, thin ugly ghost. Some people say this is the spirit of Charles Macklin, who likes to walk around the corridors and dressing rooms, before finally stopping on the spot where he killed Thomas Hallam. Maybe his spirit cannot rest, his guilt consuming his very soul.

Charles Macklin could well have been the killer of Arnold Woodruff (the man in grey) as his dates coincide with the dating of the bones found. As we can see, Mr Macklin had a furious temper when riled. Could he have been the one to plunge the dagger deep into the body of Arnold Woodruff and hide his body? What do you think?

JOSEPH GRIMALDI (1778-1837)

Another famous ghost reportedly sighted at the Theatre Royal is that of Joseph Grimaldi. Grimaldi was known as the 'father of clowns' and invented the made-up face of a clown that is so recognisable around the world today.

Joseph was a very fit and energetic man; he had to be, as his act included tumbling and acrobatics. He would perform on stage at the Theatre Royal, finish his act, then run over to the Sadler's Wells theatre and perform on that stage to a packed-out audience.

He was a dedicated artist, but sadly he didn't live to a ripe old age, as the years of his acrobatics led him to be crippled towards the end of his life.

Many actors since his death say they have felt his presence on stage with them. In fact, the story goes that if the ghost of Mr Grimaldi isn't happy with your performance, he'll give you a kick up the bum.

DAN LENO (1860-1904)

Some people report detecting the smell of lavender in the backstage area of the Theatre Royal – and this is associated with the ghost of legendary pantomime dame Dan Leno. He performed at the theatre on at least twenty occasions. He sadly died in 1904, but since then there have been several reports of seeing his ghost and smelling the sweet scent of lavender, followed by poltergeist activity backstage and in the dressing room area. I think the old pantomime dame has never stopped performing and loves nothing more than to play tricks and pranks on unsuspecting actors waiting in the wings.

One actor quite recently told his story of being alone in his dressing room when suddenly the television began to change channels of its own accord. He tried to use the remote control to stop the TV from playing up but that didn't help. He recalls feeling very spooked and was convinced that he wasn't on his own in the room. Of course, it could just be that the TV was faulty, but if I was on my own in an empty theatre at night, I think I would be more than a little scared.

THE INVESTIGATION

In 2002, I decided to investigate these hauntings myself and went with my *Most Haunted* team, equipped with our ghost-hunting kit and TV filming equipment.

This was the very first television series of *Most Haunted* that we had filmed and, as you can imagine, being allowed to spend the whole night in the world's most haunted theatre was a real coup for us. I was a beginner at ghost hunting at this point and had a lot to learn, especially about trying not to scream at every bump and thump. But I was beyond excited and very nervous, in equal measure.

Our night in this world-renowned building was one of the most memorable and spooky investigations I've ever done.

We had to wait until that night's performance of *My Fair Lady* was over. Then, once the audience, cast, crew and stage personnel had left and all the lights had been switched off, we crept into the eerily quiet and dark building. It was an amazing feeling to have the whole place to ourselves. Once the excitement had faded, we set about splitting into groups with our night-vision cameras and various pieces of ghost-hunting equipment. We were on a mission to prove the existence of these ghosts once and for all.

My first vigil was in the main auditorium. Sitting in front of a dark empty stage was a very daunting experience and one I've never forgotten. I sat in the stalls with hundreds of empty seats around me. It was deafeningly quiet and still. Thankfully, I wasn't alone because another team member had come with me. It was

pitch-black and I could only just make out the safety curtain on the stage. However, looking through a night-vision camera, all the hundreds of seats suddenly became very clear – as if someone had turned all the lights back on again.

Trust me, theatres really are quite scary when they're empty. Usually, when you sit in a theatre the sounds of applause, music and laughter are heard, so it's very odd to feel a totally different atmosphere in a place you associate with lots of people and noise.

As we sat there, suddenly, we began to get very cold, freezing in fact, which was bizarre, as there were no windows or doors open. Then I felt an icy blast of cold air being blown forcibly into my ear. That quick, unexplained action terrified me, because I felt without a doubt, that we were not alone.

I decided to call out to the ghosts that I suspected were around us. 'Is there anybody there?' I asked nervously.

Suddenly, in quick response, my colleague and I heard whispering directly behind us. It seemed to be a man's voice mumbling under his breath. We both heard it and hoped that our little camera had picked up the noise. Then the icy breath came once more; I felt it blow in my ear again. I began to physically shake with fear, imagining a man sitting behind me whispering close to my face. Whoever it was must have been aware of my fear and seemed to delight in making us scared. After a while I'd had enough and left the auditorium quickly to meet up with the rest of my *Most Haunted* team.

The next thing that happened really frightened me but at the same time cemented for ever my belief in ghosts and life after death.

I was walking down a corridor with two other members of my investigation team. We were in the upper circle of the theatre and were going to go down to the ground floor. We weren't investigating at this point and so very annoyingly didn't have a camera in our hands. We did have a camera man taking shots of us walking away though, because in the TV show we need to get lots of walking shots around the building so the audience at home can get a sense of the location. We decided to take the main staircase, which is the most beautiful feature of the whole building. Remember, it was pitch-black, and so, with only torchlight to guide the way, we headed towards the stairs.

When we reached the top of the staircase, I saw the most incredible thing – a pair of legs walking on their own up the stairs. They seemed to be moving in slow motion and what's even more bizarre and scary is that there was no *body* attached to them! I distinctly remember seeing what looked to be knee-high black boots walking by themselves.

Well, as you can imagine, all three of us turned and ran. It was freaky, frightening and very confusing. That was the first time I had seen an apparition (or part of one) in motion. I had seen a ghost a few years before and that was scary because the ghost had just stared at me; it didn't move a muscle, almost like a snapshot from a different time period. But this sighting was even better. I had so many questions: Why could we only see the legs? Who did the legs belong to? And who else had seen this bizarre ghostly apparition?

I was convinced the legs belonged to the famous ghost of the man in grey, as were my fellow investigators. The three of us had all seen the ghostly walking legs and were totally baffled. We were in shock and yet elated at the same time. It felt like someone had given us a strange gift, one that regrettably we hadn't managed to film.

My experience wasn't over yet though. Something else happened that night which remains a total mystery to this day.

I was standing in what we call the base room. This is an allocated place during a paranormal investigation where my team set up all the equipment for monitoring a haunted location. It's a room to come back to once a vigil has been completed so notes can be written up. It's also a place to catch one's breath, particularly if you've been scared half to death.

As I was talking to a fellow teammate, I was interrupted by the sound of clanking chains rattling towards us from the darkened corridor outside the base room. We both looked at each other, and I asked whether he could hear it too – he could.

At that exact moment we watched as a stout man dressed in dark clothes passed the open door holding lots of chains that rattled and clashed together as he walked. He looked solid to us, like a real person. But who was he? We both ran out of the base room to follow him but when we got into the corridor the man had simply vanished.

The whole team undertook a total search of the theatre and then called the manager on the phone to ask if there was anyone else in the building and whether there had ever been a sighting like this before.

The manager explained that no one had seen the ghost of a man fitting the description we had given him, but he also confirmed that no one else was in the theatre with us and no living person working at the theatre matched that description.

We never did find out who that man was, and I personally believe that he was indeed a ghost.

I also told the manager about the ghostly legs we had seen. The following morning, he showed me a series of recent photographs of the staircase that had been taken by an interior designer. Each shot had been taken within seconds of the next, looking from the ground floor up the staircase, and in the first couple of pictures there was nothing at all on the stairs. But then he showed me the last photograph.

In it I could clearly see the back of the figure of a man walking up the stairs. He was holding the bannister with his right hand, had a small bow in the back of his hair to keep a ponytail in place, and what's more fascinating was that he was pictured wearing over-the-knee black boots. I screeched with delight as I knew that this was the man, or rather his legs, that we had seen during our investigation.

The visit to the Theatre Royal, Drury Lane was a pure adrenalin rush for me and the investigation team. Years have now passed since I walked on that stage, but when I think about the experience, I'm more convinced than ever that the legs I saw belonged to the man in grey. Do you agree?

DID YOU KNOW?

Actors are particularly superstitious and most of the ones I know really believe in the paranormal, and many of them have had a ghostly encounter in a theatre.

I suppose William Shakespeare didn't help matters with his Scottish play, *Macbeth*. He took real curses and spells and wrote them into the script.

When the play was first produced on stage in 1606, the whole event was plagued by bad luck. The actor playing the leading lady died suddenly and so Shakespeare had to take over the role.

Throughout history, the play has been riddled with bad luck, from sudden death and actors falling off the stage, to the famous actor, Sir Laurence Olivier, narrowly dodging a falling weight from above.

Actors never call the play *Macbeth* out loud, for fear of bad luck. They call it the Scottish Play. If you are an actor in a theatre and you say the word 'Macbeth', there are certain rituals you are supposed to do to reverse the curse. You have to leave the room or area, turn around three times, spit on the floor and then ask permission to enter the room or area again. Or another actor can quote from *Hamlet*: 'Angels of grace defend us,' and that is supposed to work too!

TIVOLI VENUE

LOCATION
BUCKLEY,
WALES

THE GHOSTS
THE MAN ON
THE STAIRS

THE HANGED
MAN

PARANORMAL ACTIVITY:

VIOLENT
POLTERGEIST
ACTIVITY

BEING BURNT

SMELL OF FIRE

SEEING SMOKE

WHISTLING

VOICES

SHADOWS OF
PEOPLE

DOORS BANGING

FOOTSTEPS

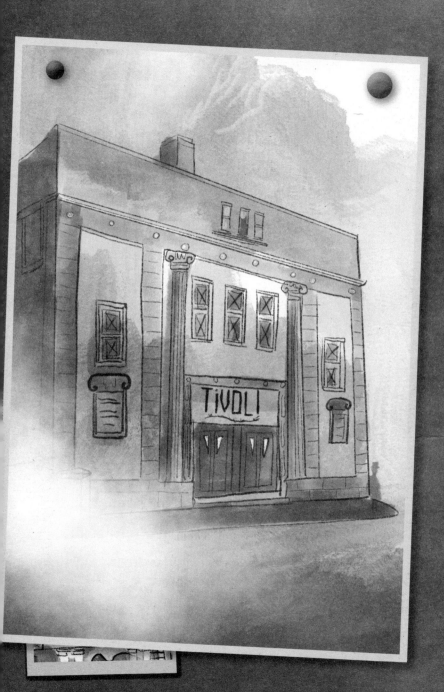

THE HISTORY

The Tivoli Venue

The Tivoli Venue was originally used from the seventeenth century as a central hall and meeting place for the locals who worked in the pottery factories and coal mines. It was also a place where huge crowds would gather to watch the spectacle of public hangings. In 1925 a cinema and music hall were built on top of where the original hall once stood, and for two decades these facilities were enjoyed by hundreds of locals from the surrounding communities.

However, in 1945 the Tivoli suffered a terrible tragedy when fire ravaged the upper floors, killing one person. A man, his identity unknown, was trapped inside the projectionist room and sadly died of smoke inhalation. The top floor of the building still bears the scars today from that dreadful event, with fire damage on the walls and ceiling. The ground floor became a popular venue for many bands, and famous names such as the Beatles, the Rolling Stones and Coldplay have all performed there.

THE HAUNTINGS

THE MAN ON THE STAIRS

No one seems sure of the identity of the unfortunate man who passed away inside the projectionist's room. Apparently, he was trapped inside as the fire blazed across the top floor. The door had somehow wedged itself shut. Was he locked inside the room on purpose, or was it an accident? Could he be the ghost that has been seen time and again walking up and down the stairs of the venue?

This strange unidentified ghost is apparently only seen when the building is shut and everyone is accounted for. On one occasion all the staff were together relaxing in the lounge area after work, waiting for a pizza to be delivered. Everyone was expecting the stage doorbell to ring when their food arrived, but to their surprise the delivery driver came straight into the room. So they asked who had let him in.

'Oh, an old man opened the door and invited me in.'

But there was no old man in the building. So, who let the pizza man in? Was it a ghost? It's certainly a mystery that to this day has never been solved.

THE HANGED MAN

Imagine working late at night and one of your jobs is to view the security footage taken by the cameras that are in every room of the Tivoli. Suddenly you see a strange image coming into focus in front of your eyes. It looks like a man, he seems to be moving, swaying almost. You look closer at the screen only to realise that you are looking at the image of a hanged man. You scrunch your eyes closed and then open them again and discover that the disturbing image has now disappeared. This is apparently what happened to one of the security guards at the Tivoli – and this terrifying vision has occurred many times to different people over the years. Who is the hanged man? No one knows. Could it be a memory of one of the public executions that took place all those hundreds of years ago on the site of the theatre?

THE INVESTIGATION

In 2015, the team and I were invited to spend the night investigating the hauntings of the Tivoli. It was in the middle of winter, cold and dark. As I got out of the car, I looked across the street at the small venue. It didn't look scary at all, in fact it almost seemed welcoming. I was keen to get started and helped the *Most Haunted* crew inside with all the cameras and ghost-hunting equipment.

For this particular investigation, I wanted to concentrate on using EVP – or Electronic Voice Phenomena. This is a way of trying to communicate with the dead that was first explored in the nineteenth century by the Spiritualist movement. Spiritualism is a religion that believes in life after death and the possibility that the living can contact the deceased. Spiritualists believe EVP is a method that allows the living to hear the voices of the dead.

An American photographer, Attila von Szalay, was allegedly the first to successfully make recordings of what he believed to be the voices of the dead in the 1900s. He made the recordings on a vinyl record to begin with, but in time this method was scrapped, and a reel-to-reel tape machine was used – giving Szalay some very haunting results. Over time he concluded that he had captured many voices, which he claimed to have come from the deceased. One such message from the other side was 'Merry Christmas and Happy New Year to you all'.

Thomas Edison, inventor of the light bulb and the motion picture camera, was a Spiritualist who believed in the afterlife. He was convinced that it was possible to talk with the dead and allegedly made drawings of a device that he called the 'Spirit Phone', a prelude to EVP. He is quoted as saying, 'I have been at work for some time building an apparatus to see if it is possible for personalities which have left this earth to communicate with us. If this is ever accomplished, it will be accomplished not by any occult, mystifying, mysterious, or weird means, such as employed by so-called "mediums" but by scientific methods.'

No one is sure if Edison ever made the phone, but if he did, I wonder what results he would have had?

Today, paranormal investigators use many different methods to try to capture voices from the dead. There are some methods I believe to be unreliable and don't use myself – such as auditory pareidolia. This is when the radio is scanning the airwaves and the investigator calls out to a spirit to 'Tell me your name'. The radio may well spew out a name, a sound or a word that has in fact simply come from a local radio station, thus making the investigator believe they are talking to that named spirit. The investigator is so desperate to get a name, they turn the noise they have just heard into the name they want to hear.

Over the years I've been lucky enough to capture remarkable evidence on various audio machines. These machines I have tried and tested along with my team. And we have discovered that going back to the basics of a reel-to-reel tape recorder delivers the best results.

So, during the investigation of the Tivoli Venue, I used a large reel-to-reel machine and a laptop ready to record any vocal anomalies. The reel-to-reel plays out what is called white noise into the atmosphere, which is the equivalent of hash on the TV. The laptop listens, waiting to pick up and record a voice from a dead person. Hopefully, a ghost answers a direct question that is asked out loud in the room.

Once our equipment was set up, I closed my eyes and concentrated, then began to call out to the spirit world, hoping that one of the ghosts allegedly haunting the Tivoli would answer, and their voice would be audible on the machines. At first nothing happened, no voice or noise could be heard but then I was alerted to the laptop screen by one of my team. Sure enough, it seemed to be picking something up. I could see one undulating wave forming on the screen. Quickly we took the curser back, highlighting the spot that signalled something had made a noise. Was it a ghostly voice?

Lo and behold, when we amplified the wave and played the sound through large speakers, we were thrilled to hear a man's gravelly voice say: 'Hello!'

I was ecstatic. To hear that voice and so quickly! The whole team was very excited and felt spurred on to investigate further. Hopefully we might find out the identities of the mysterious Tivoli ghosts.

As the dark descended upon the building, I sent two of my investigators off to the top floor, where the original auditorium was situated. With their night-vision cameras, they stalked among the crumbling stonework and fallen masonry. It wasn't long before something very spooky occurred. A heavy stone was thrown at them from the inky darkness and voices could be heard whispering words – like a hushed-up conversation was being had. Needless to say, the two investigators retreated nervously and came to join the rest of us.

On the ground floor, I had decided to begin a Ouija board session and at the same time record any words spoken on the EVP machines. A Ouija board is a fascinating piece of equipment that many believe is a way of connecting with the spirit world. The original idea was introduced as far back as 551 BC in ancient China. It became most popular during the Spiritualist movement in the 1800s.

Thanks to Hollywood and its many horror and paranormal movies, today the Ouija board is seen as a portal to the dark side, and many avoid it at all costs. Some believe that evil and mischievous spirits can come through the board and attach themselves to one or more of the sitters. I have never seen this or experienced it myself, but in truth I have had negative spirits come through, spelling out all sorts of hideous, nasty messages. But after twenty years of conducting Ouija board sessions, I can honestly say that I've never been followed home or had anything bad attach itself to me.

I always like to open a Ouija session with a quiet prayer and close the session with a small blessing. My team and I sit around a table with the board placed between us. The letters of the alphabet are printed across the middle of the board. The words 'Yes', 'No', 'Hello' and 'Goodbye' are written in each corner and a planchette or small glass is placed in the centre.

Each sitter places his or her forefinger on top of the planchette or glass and then one person begins to ask the spirits to come towards us and give a message by moving the glass over to certain letters, to either form a name or a message.

I remember my first time doing this and I was shaking with nerves but curious to see what would happen and whether we would communicate with a dead person. It wasn't long before the small glass began to vibrate and then it shot off to the word 'Hello'.

I'll never forget that nerve-wracking experience and, even now, I get excited when I attend a Ouija session.

So, who would we contact now at the Tivoli Venue? Sitting comfortably around a circular table, my team and I placed our fingers on an upturned drinking glass. One investigator sat on the stage next to the EVP machine. Hopefully a ghost would come through and talk on the board and simultaneously use the EVP.

I began by asking the board to move the glass to 'Yes' if there was a spirit with us. Straight away, the glass moved towards the three-letter word.

I asked, 'Do you belong to this building?' Immediately we all heard a man's voice come out of the speaker of the radio saying, 'Yes' and instantaneously the glass went back over to the word 'Yes'.

Nervously, I inquired, 'Do you haunt this place?' Again, the glass slid quickly over to the word 'Yes' and at that exact moment we again heard the deep voice of a man say 'Yes'.

So I asked his name.

Straight away the word came back through the speakers as the glass rolled over some letters. The voice said 'Ha . . . rry' and the Ouija board confirmed the same name.

I then pushed on to ask when and where Harry had died, and to our amazement he confirmed that he had indeed perished in the fire of 1945. I wanted to ask more. Was he the ghost seen on the stairs? Was he the man who died in the projectionist's room? But suddenly all communication stopped, which of course was highly frustrating for us all.

I wanted more answers, so I instructed my team to split up. I went into the projectionist's room with three other team members and sure enough, through the laptop, Harry was happy to talk to us again. When asked if he had died in the projectionist's chair, a quick response came back with a very strong Northern accent: 'No!'

I called out again and again to Harry, urging him, cajoling him to manifest himself to us. Would he come out of the shadows and walk the stairs once more?

As I continued to talk to the ghost of Harry, another team member downstairs saw what he described as a dark shadow flitting behind the bar. He walked towards the area, wanting to see who it was, but as he got closer, he became very emotional. I arrived downstairs to see him crying. I was very concerned and asked him what was wrong.

'When I got close to the dark shadow,' he replied, 'I heard a voice in my ear, and it said "Stop!" Then the voice continued to whisper, "Get out now before you die!"'

As you can imagine, the experience had terrified and distressed him.

An hour or so
went by and during
that time every member
of my investigation team
experienced poltergeist activity.
More stones were thrown, we
heard more whistling and oddly
enough we also heard a piano playing
even though there was no piano in
the building any more. But perhaps
the best moment for me was actually
seeing for myself the ghost of the man
on the stairs – who I now call Harry.

I had been asking and asking for the ghost to
come back and speak to me and, boy, did I get
the fright of my life when I saw a man in dark
shadow lean around the wall at the top of the
stairs and stare at me. I screamed in fright at first

but then swallowed my fear and chased after him. Round and round I went, down the stone steps, hoping to see the back of the man I had just encountered. I, and two other members of my team, then heard the doors bang open and close. But when we got to the bottom there was no one there. We searched everywhere, went out onto the street, but there was no sign of the man we had just seen. However, I had asked the ghost of Harry to show himself and I believe he had done just that.

But the night wasn't yet over as one brave team member decided to go it alone in the gents' toilets. This was a part of the building where poltergeist activity had been reported in the past, especially behind the bar area. Glasses had apparently been regularly thrown at staff working late, and they all complained of being narrowly missed by a glass projectile that luckily smashed on the floor and not their head.

Our courageous colleague sat in the quietness of the gents' toilets under the hand dryer. But he was shaken to the core when a tap suddenly turned on all by itself. He got up to investigate and saw that the taps were push-down mechanisms and needed force to get them to work. Who had turned it on? The investigator sat back down and took a deep breath but soon sprang up again in fear as the hand dryer went off just above his head. In fact, this happened twice, and the poor investigator can be seen on camera physically shaking. This was not a dryer that responded to movement; like the taps it was a push-button mechanism that needed someone to press it in order for it to work.

Our final vigil that evening was to be held in the cellar, where again poltergeist activity had been reported. Would we experience any as we walked around in the pitch dark? We were all nervous and a little excited, as so much had happened to us already that evening. What could we encounter now? Down in the cellar there were all sorts of items precariously placed on shelves and positioned on the floor: old oil cans, screwdrivers and light bulbs.

Suddenly, an almighty *SMASH!* shattered the silence. Everyone screamed and jumped. Catching our breath, we began to look around to see what could have made the noise – and then we found it. A single light bulb lay broken and splintered on the floor. That really could have hurt someone, so I decided that we needed to get out, as I wasn't about to let any of my investigators get injured. We left the cellar.

Although we never did find out about the hanged man, we were all convinced that the man on the stairs was called Harry and had been the projectionist who was killed in 1945. I know I saw his ghost and I will never forget that image of him staring at me.

THE OLD NICK THEATRE

LOCATION

GAINSBOROUGH, LINCOLNSHIRE

GHOSTS

POLTERGEISTS

THE FACELESS POLICEMEN

PARANORMAL ACTIVITY

POLTERGEIST ACTIVITY

FURNITURE BEING THROWN AND MOVED

PEOPLE BEING PUSHED ON THE STAIRS

SLAMMING OF DOORS

SOUNDS OF MEN AND WOMEN CRYING AND SOBBING

FOOTSTEPS HEARD

WHISTLING AND KEYS JANGLING

THE HISTORY

The Old Nick

The Old Nick Theatre sits on the corner of two converging roads in Gainsborough, Lincolnshire. This building was built in 1860 as the headquarters for the Lincolnshire constabulary and the magistrates' court. In its time this Victorian police station, small prison and court tried and convicted thousands of men and women – some guilty, some innocent.

In 1974 the police moved to a different building, and in 1979 the Old Nick was then converted into a theatre and police museum. The first floor, which had been the magistrates' court where people were tried for their crimes, was turned into a small intimate theatre and dressing room area. This is the only part of the building that has really altered. The prison cells on the ground floor remain untouched, as does the main reception hall, the watch room, and offices.

As you walk around the building there are still signs of its old occupants. Graffiti from the early twentieth century can be seen scratched into walls and on the back of cell doors, a grisly reminder of lives lived in a more brutal and unsympathetic time.

The Gainsborough Theatre Company now owns the building and has reported that the property is haunted. Some members are too scared to enter the building alone, day or night. When I heard a couple of their stories, I just had to bring my team and experience this place for myself.

THE HAUNTINGS

POLTERGEISTS

I always feel sorry for the people who have to lock up late at night in these haunted locations. Imagine being the one to walk around an old theatre, armed with only your torch for safety and reassurance as you make your way through an ancient building that seems to be alive with the spirits of the dead.

One poor woman had just started her new job at the theatre. It was her first day and as she headed towards the auditorium, she heard talking and laughter. As she climbed the stairs, the voices got louder and louder, but when she entered the auditorium, she was shocked to discover there was no one there. The auditorium was completely empty. Then, to the poor woman's horror, she heard what she described as heavy furniture being dragged around on the floor. She didn't hang around to find out what was causing that phenomenon, she just fled in abject terror. But on the way out, she witnessed a table lift off the floor and fly through the air before landing with an almighty crash in the corner of the room!

Another reported incident involved two actors who were apparently rehearsing a scene in a play late one night. When they came to the last word, which was 'murderer', all three doors flew open at the same time with a terrifying whoosh. A sudden, perfectly-timed gust of wind? Or the response of a poltergeist?

THE FACELESS POLICEMEN

Downstairs in the Old Nick Theatre, in the area where the police worked, many people have claimed to hear footsteps, whistling and the jangling of keys. Witnesses have also described seeing a dark shadow or two, and even the outline of a police uniform has been glimpsed,

but never a face. These dark shadows don't want to show themselves and I believe they could be memories rather than actual ghosts.

THE INVESTIGATION

When the team and I arrived for this particular investigation one night in 2015, we decided to split up into smaller groups straight away and I sent two investigators down into the male prisoners' cells. With no natural light from the streetlights outside, the corridor leading to the cells was as black as tar. Shining their torches, they made their way slowly and carefully down the dark stone corridor and into one of the small cells. But as soon as they entered the claustrophobic room, feelings of oppression and depression came over them both. Suddenly, a loud bang ricocheted down the corridor and both men ran out to see what had made the noise. They looked at each cell door and discovered one was firmly shut. Without knowing if the door had always been closed, they couldn't say for certain that was the noise they had just heard. Trying it themselves, they opened and slammed the cell door and realised that was exactly the noise they'd just heard. But who could have closed it and with such force? The two investigators were now convinced they were not on their own.

As they made their way back to the first cell, they heard the sound of furniture being moved inside it. But they both knew the cell was empty. And then, suddenly, loud whistling stopped the ghost hunters in their tracks. They stood dead still and stared wildly at each other. Yes, they'd both heard it.

Luckily, this audio phenomenon was caught on camera. The sound is clear and eerie. When I watch the footage back, it gives me the creeps.

Meanwhile, I had decided that being the only woman on the team that night, it was probably a good idea if I spent some time inside the women's cells. I didn't go alone. I took with me two other investigators, and, as soon as I started to call out to see if there were any female spirits with us, we all heard faint tapping and knocking noises. We couldn't tell where the strange sounds were coming from. The walls? The floor? The ceiling? The knocking and tapping were constant, faint but definitely audible.

I asked out loud, 'Would you like to talk to us?' and in response we all heard a woman's pitiful, moaning cry. Terrifying!

Meanwhile, back in the men's cells, the two investigators had now both heard a loud and unnerving scream. Where or who had it come

from? They quickly made their way out of the cell they were standing in and stumbled in the direction of where they thought the deathly scream had come from. Sure enough, after a few steps, another cell door slammed shut in front of them. The noise was deafening, and instantly whistling and tapping could be heard throughout the whole area. The two investigators were now one hundred per cent convinced that there were multiple spirits playing with them. But even though the two ghost hunters could hear the doors slamming, the whistling and crying, they didn't see any ghostly apparitions. The faceless ghosts of the prisoners seemed to want to stay incognito. But if their intention was to scare the investigators, they had clearly achieved their goal.

The cells and corridors on the ground floor were certainly a hot bed of paranormal activity, but what about the old magistrates' court upstairs, where a bad-tempered poltergeist allegedly liked to throw furniture about? I was keen to get up the stairs and find out if this temperamental ghost would greet us.

The room upstairs was quite small and dark, with a square stage where actors would perform to their audience who sat in old cinema seats along the back of the room.

I had now gathered all my investigators together and we stood in the centre of the stage, soaking up the atmosphere, waiting for something to happen. Within a few moments some of the *Most Haunted* team began to complain of dizziness. It's quite common for one person perhaps to feel a little dizzy or even sick in a haunted location, but for the whole team to feel this way was quite unusual.

I thought that it must somehow be due to the atmosphere and the spirits that were surrounding us.

I took my cue and began to call out, asking for whoever was here with us to make themselves known and come out of the shadows to communicate.

Straight away, knocking and tapping could be heard pounding underneath the seating area. Suddenly, one of the investigators cried out and pointed with a shaky hand to the corner of the room. He claimed he'd just seen the figure of a man.

By now, we had all moved to the seating area and could hear and feel the tapping and knocking coming through the floor. It was so loud and forceful it actually made me jump and cry out in shock. And then a most ominous noise began. The vibrations started to form a pattern. It sounded like a human heart pounding continuously. Da . . . dum, da . . . dum, da . . . dum.

'How many spirits are with us now?' I asked out loud and immediately the pounding grew louder. Then, like a horse charging off into the distance, the strange, haunting noise dissipated.

'That's a lot,' one of my team replied nervously. Then someone in the team screamed and fell backwards. He described seeing a shadowy figure with eyes, a nose, and dark features.

I asked for this ghost to show itself so we could all witness it. We waited, holding our breath and then without warning a door in the room slammed shut.

I spun round, and as I did so, I felt a deep breath in my ear. I froze momentarily with terror, but taking a beat, I swallowed down my fear and told my companions what I had just experienced. No one else had felt it.

Suddenly, footsteps could clearly be heard walking across the stage, before the squeaking, grinding sound of the auditorium seats began to echo all around us. They were being moved, but not by any of us. Was it some unseen force? The sound of a seat slamming down into its open position sent us all into a frenzy, searching the area to see which one had been moved. We found an open seat, a seat which needs the weight of someone sitting on it to keep it open. But there was no one there. Was there a ghost sitting on it that we couldn't see? We asked for the ghosts to move it again. But after waiting several minutes, we were disappointed as the seat stubbornly didn't seem to want to move back into its original upright position.

One investigator then suggested he would go alone to the warden's room by the women's cells, thinking that being a man, the female ghosts might react to having some male company.

The investigator headed downstairs and along the lonely dark corridor, entering the small office and sitting at the desk. He called out and waited for a response – and he wasn't disappointed. He clearly heard – and the noise is captured on camera – a woman's voice saying, 'Excuse me'. Then much to the investigator's fright, the desk moved all on its own and slid a few feet away from him.

As you can imagine, this was a frightening situation to be in and if I had been on my own, I would have shot out of there as quickly as possible. But this investigator was very brave and stayed sitting in his seat calling out to the ghost and asking if she would move the desk again. Then the most extraordinary thing happened: the desk did move – again and again. It moved on command two more times. All this evidence was caught on our cameras and makes for some intriguing and frightening viewing. The lone investigator was now satisfied that he had captured enough footage of this astounding exchange and got out of there as quickly as possible.

This incredible location was, to a paranormal investigator, the best of both worlds, a haunted theatre *and* an old prison. All those energies rolled into one building; how could we not capture some kind of paranormal activity? I have to admit though, a part of me felt a little disappointed by the investigation, as I had really wanted to get a name, or an identity for some of the ghosts that reside there. Who slammed the doors to the cells? And what was the name of the ghostly lady who asked one investigator to 'Excuse me'?

DID YOU KNOW?

The lights at the front of the stage, known as footlights, are thought to have been positioned in such a way so as to stop actors from falling off the edge of the stage and hurting themselves. Also, they add that extra bit of illumination so the audience can see the cast more clearly. But there is another reason why the footlights are placed there. Many believe that they are positioned to ward off negative, evil spirits and bad falls and broken bones. Well, after discovering some of the accidents that have occurred on many stages, these mythical ghost lights don't seem to have done a very good job, have they?

MORECAMBE WINTER GARDENS

LOCATION

MORECAMBE, LANCASHIRE

THE GHOSTS

THE ARCHITECTS

THE WOMAN
ON THE STAIRS

THE WARDROBE MISTRESS

THE WOMAN IN UNIFORM

THE MANAGER
ON THE STAGE

THE DEVILISH CLOWN

UNKNOWN DARK FIGURES

PARANORMAL ACTIVITY

VIOLENT POLTERGEIST
ACTIVITY

INTENSE HEAT AND
HOT SPOTS

OBJECTS THROWN
AND MOVED WITH
VIOLENCE

MOANS AND CRIES
HEARD REGULARLY

REPORTED FEELINGS
OF NAUSEA AND
DIZZINESS

GROWLING

COLD AIR BLOWN IN
FACE OR EAR

FOOTSTEPS HEARD
REGULARLY

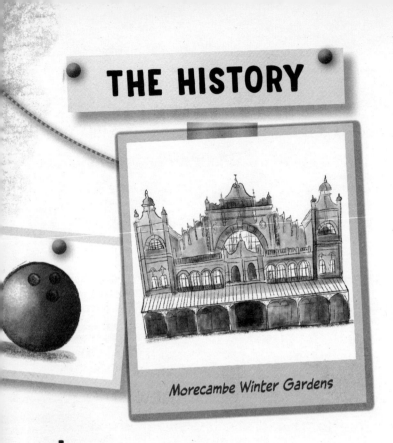

Morecambe Winter Gardens

In the late nineteenth century, architects William Mangnall and William Littlewood constructed the large and impressive Morecambe Winter Gardens theatre. It is a beautiful building that stands where the local seawater baths were once situated. It was one of the largest theatres in the country and designed to be the grandest music hall that audiences had ever seen. It had five bars and an open promenade area, allowing the well-to-do society of the day to see who was at the theatre and, more importantly, with whom.

During World War Two, like many large buildings, Morecambe Winter Gardens was requisitioned by the armed forces for training purposes. After the war, its theatre days were numbered because the popularity of television had driven many theatre lovers away. They now preferred to sit and watch a small box in the corner of their front room. Why dress up and go outside to be entertained when they could sit, relax and be entertained from their own homes?

Slowly but surely the theatre began to lose its audiences and it was eventually changed from a theatre into a cinema. But by 1977 that too had lost its appeal and the Morecambe Winter Gardens theatre closed its doors for a final time. It is now owned by the Friends of the Winter Gardens, who are determined to return it to its former glory one day.

THE HAUNTINGS

For many years there have been reports of an imaginary line drawn through the theatre. This line allegedly separates the good side from the dark side.

Let's begin with the good side and its alleged ghosts.

THE ARCHITECTS

The architects Mangnall and Littlewood are said to haunt their old offices. Even though they mean no harm, it's believed they don't particularly like strangers entering their space. The two gentlemen loved the place so much that they have refused to leave, even after death. Their ghosts have been seen wandering the whole building. Sometimes it's said they appear as a mist; others describe a full apparition.

THE WOMAN ON THE STAIRS

The ghost of an unknown Edwardian lady is said to haunt the dress circle and one particular grand staircase. No one knows for sure what connection she had with the theatre, but it is claimed that the poor woman died after falling down the stairs. There is a mystery surrounding her death. Was she pushed, or did she stumble and fall?

Apparently, so the story goes, late one evening she was overheard having an argument with her married lover. Shouting was heard, followed suddenly by a loud scream, and then silence.

When questioned, her lover insisted that she fell as she ran down the stairs, but there are still many who believe she was pushed, falling tragically to her death.

When her ghost is seen on the stairs, some witnesses claim the whole scene is played out before them as if the ghost is trying to tell them something.

THE WARDROBE MISTRESS

In the dressing rooms, the spectre of a wardrobe mistress has been seen on numerous occasions. It's thought that she was a failed dancer and now, through her bitterness and anger, she haunts relentlessly, whimpering and crying over her disappointing career.

THE WOMAN IN UNIFORM

Another ghost which has been seen in the theatre is that of a woman dressed in RAF uniform. She's harmless enough but apparently doesn't like to interact with people, and when she is seen, she quickly fades away.

THE MANAGER ON THE STAGE

Now we move on to the dark side of the theatre and all of its ghostly inhabitants. Firstly, there is said to be the apparition of a former theatre manager, who people have reported encountering. His ghost is only seen on the stage. This spook is very frightening because according to witnesses, if he doesn't like the look of you, he's been known to violently punch, kick and slap people.

THE DEVILISH CLOWN

It is reported that staircase number two is plagued by the entity of a most malevolent spirit, who is known to follow and terrorise people. Most witnesses describe him as a small person, who perhaps could have worked as an actor or a clown on the stage. His energy carries violence and anger, and apparently this spirit loves nothing more than to physically attack people and throw stones, nuts, bolts and screws at them.

UNKNOWN DARK FIGURES

Down in the basement of the Winter Gardens, there is a maze of dark rooms. Shadowy figures have been seen cowering in the murkiest of corners and it's rumoured that they are hiding from something far more sinister than themselves. But what?

THE INVESTIGATION

THE GOOD SIDE

When I investigated this theatre, I wanted to concentrate on the 'good' side of the building first. So, my team and I set up our cameras in the area that fascinated me most: the staircase where the Edwardian lady had met her tragic demise.

I had invited psychic artist and good friend, Brian Shepherd, to join me in this vast theatre. Not only can Brian talk to spirits from the other side, but he can sketch them too. It's phenomenal how he can scribble on paper, drawing with his charcoal pencil the ghosts that come into his mind.

Brian's talent is incredible and he's the psychic I most trust and believe. There are many people like Brian who can draw or paint spirits from the other side, and it's a remarkable gift and one to behold if you find the right person.

Brian really convinced me of his psychic skills back in 2008, when we were filming *Most Haunted* and investigating Sleepy Hollow Cemetery in America.

I had just flown in from the UK after my dad's funeral and, as you can imagine, a cemetery was the last place I wanted to be. I was very emotional and tired. Brian came over to me, put his arm around my shoulders and whispered, 'Your dad's here with you and he's saying thank you for putting the hat and flag in his coffin. He loved it.'

I was astounded. No one, not even my husband Karl, knew about the items I had placed inside my dad's coffin.

Then Brian added, 'Your dad's asking you to spread his ashes at the Trafalgar.'

I was confused. 'What is the Trafalgar?'

'I don't know,' said Brian, 'but he just keeps repeating it, over and over.'

Well, after that and a few phone calls back home, I discovered what the Trafalgar was. It was an English pub that my dad loved to frequent in Miami, USA. This was something I hadn't known about but when I found it out, I was blown away.

What I love about Brian is that he doesn't talk about his gift, and he doesn't charge any money for his sketches. He does it to help people. So, when he said he could join us for this particular investigation, we were all thrilled.

Anyway, back to the Morecambe Winter Gardens and its many ghosts.

Once we had established ourselves on the staircase where the Edwardian lady is often seen, we waited with bated breath to see if she would appear to us. It was pitch-black and very cold, and our whispered voices echoed around the marble staircase and the foyer below. Brian began to talk softly, calling out for the woman to come closer, and after a short while we all heard what could only be described as moaning. A woman's voice was reverberating distinctly around us all. I looked at the sound man and he nodded that he had indeed heard the noise and managed to record it.

I asked Brian if he could see anything. He squeezed his eyes closed in concentration and went into a trance-like state, beginning to talk quietly.

'There's an intense energy here. Something occurred on these stairs. I can see her. She's a lady who wears long skirts. I can see a couple saying goodbye to one another.' Brian's voice became more urgent, his arm outstretched as if trying to hold something. He whispered, 'She stumbles, and her body is crumpled at the bottom. She's haunting these stairs because of the traumatic way in which she passed over.'

Suddenly, as if in agreement, there was another whimper, then one more groan was heard by us all.

'Was she pushed, Brian?'

I asked. The whimpering was getting louder now, and we were all looking worried and afraid.

'No, she wasn't pushed, she . . . fell. Her feet became caught up in her long skirts and she fell.'

My team of investigators and I managed to record some of our best ghostly vocal phenomena to date on that marble staircase. I feel sure that the ghost was listening to our conversation, and by her sighs, cries and moans, was letting us know that what Brian was saying was true.

After that, I decided to move up to the first floor and the architects' office. Of course, the space looks nothing like an office now. Sparse brick walls and a concrete floor were all that greeted us as we entered the small, dark space.

As soon as Brian walked inside the room,

he blurted out that the smell of paper was very strong, and no sooner had he spoken than a large block of wood hit me on the shoulder. I screamed with shock. Where this had come from, no one knew. And this was supposed to be the good side of the theatre!

Brian went on to describe two male ghosts who he said were standing in the room with us, and he confirmed that yes, they were architects, naming each one correctly: Mr Mangnall and Mr Littlewood.

'They don't want us in here,' he said.

Out of respect for the ghosts and their privacy, I ushered my team away from the room and then moved everyone up into the dressing room area.

This was where the ghost of a wardrobe mistress had been seen. Surely nothing bad could happen in this part of the theatre, could it? But how wrong I was. Within seconds of us all standing together in the dark, a long, loud, deep moan was heard.

'This is a dancer,' shouted Brian excitedly.

Then in an instant I heard a woman gently singing. It was incredibly eerie. The sound was in the vicinity of where we were all standing but we couldn't tell exactly where it was coming from. Again, the sound man nodded to say he had recorded the spooky phenomenon and I have played it back and listened to it many times.

I began to call out, hoping that the wardrobe mistress or dancer would talk to us and that I would catch a glimpse of a shadowy figure.

Suddenly a piece of masonry was thrown at Brian.

No one was quite certain where it had come from. Once we had checked that Brian was all right, I continued to call out.

'If that was you throwing stuff, can you do it again or make another noise?' I asked. I was answered rather unpleasantly. For the next few minutes, we were bombarded with disgusting growls and grunts. Sometimes in our ears, other times close to the microphones. I didn't like what I was hearing.

Who was doing this and why? We wanted some answers and so I decided to conduct a Ouija board session. Hopefully we would get the name of the wardrobe mistress, and that way find out who was responsible for the growling. What spirit would come through and talk to us? I was apprehensive and excited, as I knew the rest of my colleagues were.

Brian sat in the corner of the dressing room, his paper and charcoal at the ready, whilst I and the rest

of my team sat around the Ouija board table. When I called out for the glass to move over the letters, Brian would sketch the spirits that had drawn close to us all.

Within a few moments of me calling out and asking for a response, the table began to shake. The only way I can describe it is, imagine if you were to put your hand on top of a washing machine on a spin cycle; that's the vibrating feeling you get when the right energy comes through. It's incredible. I then asked for the name of the wardrobe mistress, and sure enough, the glass spelled out 'Anne'.

I whispered, 'Were you a dancer?' The glass slid quickly over to the word 'Yes'.

Pushing on, I asked, 'Was that you we heard singing earlier?' Again, the glass moved urgently and with certainty over to the word 'Yes'.

Meanwhile Brian was scribbling away, his hand moving quickly, eyes closed, his face a picture of concentration. Suddenly he stood up and said to me, 'There's something right next to you, Yvette.

A female figure.' He paused, staring into a space to my left. I looked slowly and gingerly to where he was gazing and then glanced back at Brian. He smiled and said, 'It's not Anne. She's over there. I can see another figure standing beside you, and this one's protecting you.'

'Who is it?' I asked.

'It's your grandma. She's always beside you, protecting you in case a spirit gets too close.'

I looked at the sketch Brian had been doing and suddenly I was overcome with emotion because I could see the image of my grandma standing over me with her hand on my shoulder. Brian had never met my grandma or seen a photograph of her and yet the likeness in his drawing was uncanny.

BRIAN'S DRAWING

After a little break, I decided to go with just two other investigators back up to the architects' office, with the hope of experiencing some more poltergeist activity from the two gentlemen's spirits. I had urged the team to leave earlier out of respect for their space, but I hoped that with just three people present they might be a little more welcoming.

I decided to call out their names and introduce myself. Maybe they would say their names out loud or perhaps throw something else. Instead, we managed to capture the ghostly sound of slow, heavy footsteps walking towards us. My fellow investigators and I grabbed each other, entwined in fear as the footsteps came into the room. They seemed to walk around us, as if looking at us, perhaps sizing us up, and then they stopped as suddenly as they'd begun.

THE DARK SIDE

It was imperative that we now investigated the dark side of the theatre. Although we were pleased with the paranormal activity we had captured already, what more would we witness on the dark side?

I wanted to start on the second staircase where the evil entity of a small person had been seen and felt. We all crowded in the middle of the stairs, our cameras pointing in various directions. The sound man was ready with his boom mic, keen to capture more unexplained sounds.

Brian looked worried and turned to me and said he had a bad feeling and sense of foreboding in the place. 'Something is rushing up and down these stairs. It's a small person, an act from the stage. Whoever it is, he's aggressive.'

Nervously, I moved us all up to the dress circle of the theatre. Brian then continued to tell us all that a very negative spirit was trying to get us all out. 'He's very violent and is shouting profanities at the women on the stage,' he said.

Suddenly a stone was thrown, and it landed on one of the investigator's heads. He shouted out in pain, then another stone was lobbed at a crew member, and they too screamed out in fright.

'Careful now,' said Brian. 'He's trying to get you out, he's very angry.' Brian scrunched his eyes shut tight and then yelled out a man's name, relief obviously rushing through him at getting an identity.

Brian told us that the ghost's name was Stan, and he was apparently very attached to the ghost of a woman who used to work at the theatre. Brian could see her walking down the aisles selling sweets and cigarettes, and Stan adored her.

Straight away, another member of the team was hit by a flying object, and then another investigator nearly fell over, and said that something had just grabbed her leg.

It was clear my investigators were being targeted and someone could get seriously hurt. I was concerned. I didn't want anyone being taken off to hospital. That had happened before during quite a few investigations, and I didn't want there to be another incident tonight.

I suggested we give the area a rest and move onto somewhere else, and everyone happily agreed. So we pressed on down into the basement.

What a terrible place that was: an enormous, pitch-black space. A warren of dark rooms that were empty and very cold. Just when we thought we had looked in every room, another one seemed to pop up out of the darkness. We certainly didn't have to wait long before something paranormal occurred.

To begin with we could all hear a rumbling sound but couldn't quite work out where the noise was coming from. Then suddenly: *BANG!*

I screamed as something heavy landed in the middle of us all.

We switched on our torches and found, to our amazement, a large blue bowling ball, slowly rolling to a stop. I decided that we needed to get out of the area as I could tell the paranormal activity was becoming more dangerous with every passing second.

This incredible location had given us lots to think about and loads of paranormal footage for us to view at a later date. I was overjoyed that Brian had been able provide us with more information about the ghosts that were haunting the building. And of course, we had his wonderful sketches.

If you ever have the chance to visit this amazing theatre, then you must go. You won't be disappointed, but remember to tread carefully on the stairs!

DID YOU KNOW?

The nickname for a clown is 'Joey'. This name comes from the father of clowns, the nineteenth-century pantomime actor Joseph Grimaldi. You should recognise his name as you will now know he graced the stage at the Theatre Royal, Drury Lane.

The word 'clown' derives from an Icelandic word, klunni, which means a clumsy person, something which the ghost of the clown running up and down the stairs at the Morecambe Winter Gardens certainly isn't. But he's definitely not afraid to trip up an unsuspecting visitor.

THE LYCEUM THEATRE

GHOSTS
THE LADY IN WHITE
CHARLIE THE STAGEHAND
A DEMONIC ENTITY
A LOST CHILD
A HOODED FIGURE

LOCATION
CREWE, CHESHIRE

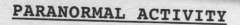

PARANORMAL ACTIVITY
POLTERGEIST ACTIVITY
DOORS SLAMMING
WHISTLING
SINGING
OBJECTS DISAPPEARING
OBJECTS THROWN

OUIJ
EFGI
RSTU
3456

THE HISTORY

The Lyceum Theatre

The Lyceum Theatre Crewe was built on top of an old Roman Catholic church and graveyard. The church was built for Irish immigrants who had come over to England to help build the railways in that part of the country. Then, in 1852, a famous actor of the day – Henry Taylor – began working on his dream to create a beautiful theatre on the site.

In 1885 Henry Taylor and his friend Alfred Darbyshire completed their mission of constructing a 1500-seat auditorium, complete with a working well in the cellar right under the stage. This well had belonged to the church, and the original foundations of that religious building can still be seen today.

As with all theatres, Crewe Lyceum has certainly had its fair share of stars tread its boards, but two of the most famous were masters of comedy: Charlie Chaplin (who performed in a production of *Sherlock Holmes*) and Stan Laurel – one half of Laurel and Hardy (who appeared there in a production of *Sleeping Beauty*).

However, in 1910 the theatre tragically caught fire. Flames ravaged through the whole building, completely destroying Henry Taylor's beautiful theatre. No one knows for sure what or who could have caused the fire, but a cigarette butt was discovered in one of the dressing rooms.

A friend of Henry's and another famous actor of the time, Edward Compton, stepped in to help build a replacement, and by 1911 a new theatre had been constructed, the one we see today.

THE HAUNTINGS

THE LADY IN WHITE

For the past fifty years, the ghost of a lady dressed in white has reportedly been seen regularly in the Lyceum and is believed to be the spirit of a ballerina who tragically took her own life in one of the dressing rooms. Her name was Annie Edwards and her ghost is always accompanied by the smell of lavender. Her ghost is seen most often in the dress circle seating area but has been witnessed in the dressing room area too.

CHARLIE THE STAGEHAND

A playful entity is said to lurk on the stage and in the wings. This ghost has been given the nickname 'Charlie' by those working in the theatre, and apparently loves nothing more than to hide props and objects.

A DEMONIC ENTITY

There is also believed to be a demonic and menacing spirit causing mayhem and unease all over the theatre, particularly on and around the stage. Could this dark spirit perhaps have caused the devastating fire back in 1910?

According to records, at one point the ghostly activity became unbearable and so in 1969 an exorcist was called in to help. But whatever was done failed to alleviate the ghostly phenomena and so the problematic hauntings have continued to this day.

THE INVESTIGATION

It was 2016 when we investigated this location. When we arrived, the lights were off throughout the building and an eerie silence had descended. I gathered my team of investigators together and suggested we begin our night on the stage. If the mischievous spirit, nicknamed Charlie, liked to play games, then I was eager to see if he'd introduce himself to us. Standing apart from each other, looking out into the inky blackness where an audience was usually waiting to be entertained, we whispered amongst ourselves about how intrigued and nervous we felt.

One investigator mumbled, 'I feel like we're all being watched,' and sure enough, as if something *were* observing us, a noise was heard coming from inside one of the elaborate theatre boxes.

Then another team member suddenly shouted out: 'There!'

Pointing up to the box, he whispered that he'd just seen a figure, a shadow moving in the box where the noise was coming from.

We all agreed that the noise we had heard sounded like the rustling of clothing, as though someone were getting up to walk away. So we stood on the stage, staring silently at the box, waiting to see or hear something else. After a few minutes had passed I began to call out: 'Come and talk to us.' Nothing. 'Can you copy me?' I said, and whistled a little tune into the deathly quietness. And we were all astounded when a whistle came straight back.

Our excitement was growing as it became more obvious that something or someone was present.

I encouraged the spirit or spirits to come closer, make more noises perhaps. It wasn't long before my invitation was accepted. Loud thudding and tapping noises emanated from the seating area and then gradually came onto the front of the stage. Then the sounds began to move all around us, as if some person were sussing us all out. Eventually, just as quickly as the noises had begun, they faded into the distance, taking a stage exit.

I asked who in the team now wanted to go off on their own, perhaps down into the cellar where the ancient water well and old foundations of the church were still visible. Would this brave volunteer come face to face with a ghostly hooded figure who others had reported seeing, or something far more terrible?

One of the team did agree to go, and went off into the darkness, armed only with a night-vision camera and nerves of steel. Meanwhile the rest of us stayed on the stage, keen to draw out any of the other ghostly entities. We positioned a Ouija board on a table in the centre of the stage and hoped that whatever spiritual entity was present would move the glass towards the letters on the board and give us some information. We sat around the table and began.

'If you're here,' I shouted, 'then do something, make a noise, use your voice, talk to us, throw something.' My voice bounced around the empty theatre. We all sat with  our fingers on the glass nervously waiting for some kind of response, and it wasn't long before we got the shock of our lives . . .

Down in the murky cellar, the lone investigator had begun to walk through the narrow corridors that led to several small rooms, asking the spirits to come and make themselves known to him. Soon he and the camera picked up a loud *BANG!* One of the doors had slammed shut on its own. With no breeze down in the cellar this was enough to set the poor man on edge.

Back on the stage, I had decided to call out to the ghost of the ballerina: 'Annie Edwards, are you here?'

Almost immediately the sound of running feet echoed all around us and then suddenly a deafening smashing sound made us all jump up from our seats in terror.

'What the hell was that?' shouted one team member. All our torches went on and we began searching the area and backstage, desperately trying to find what had smashed on the floor. It took us a while but eventually we found it. As I was walking about in the wings, I felt something crunch under my feet and there to my surprise were the remains of a light-bulb filament. Shards of broken glass lay all around me. I knew the glass wasn't there before as we would have noticed it when we walked onto the stage. But the weirdest thing was the filament was hot to the touch even though the light hadn't been on. Where had it come from and who had thrown it?

Meanwhile, the poor lone investigator deep in the cellar was having the life scared out of him too, as yet another door slammed with force. Feeling vulnerable, the investigator decided to leave the cellar and go up to one of the dressing rooms.

This dressing room wasn't the one the ballerina had allegedly killed herself in, but it was a room that the investigator felt compelled to go into. It was small and dark, with a chair positioned in front of a mirror set against a wall. There was a cupboard where coat hangers tinkled against each other as he arrived. But other than that, all seemed quiet and quite normal. Suddenly the investigator felt uneasy and emotional, although he couldn't explain why.

Before long a scratching noise was heard coming from the other side of the door. He went to it and opened it slowly. Satisfied there was nothing there, he closed the door. As he sat back down in the chair, something was thrown at him without warning. Quickly he turned his torch on and began to look around for the object that had been launched, but to his amazement there was nothing there.

Shaking now, the investigator called out and asked for whatever or whoever was with him to throw something again. On cue another object was thrown, and you can clearly hear on the footage of the investigation an object bouncing around the room. To me it sounds like a snooker ball, but yet again when the investigator tried to find the evidence, there was nothing there.

The investigator backed himself into the corner of the room, frightened by what else might come his way. Fortunately, or unfortunately, whichever way you choose to look at it, something else was fired at him.

The footage caught something falling from the ceiling and hitting the investigator. When we slowed the footage down, it looked like a shiny sliver of something; something sharp, possibly a knife. What that object was though, we can only guess, because again nothing was found. But you can definitely hear and see it being thrown from above on the footage.

Back on the stage, everyone was huddled together, examining the EVP. We had set up the radio and laptop on the stage, in the hope of capturing any ghostly auditory phenomena. As we scanned the wave forms on the laptop and listened, we stumbled across a very strange demonic voice, recorded just after the light bulb was smashed. No one had heard the noise with their own ears but here on the EVP, it was clear for everyone to decipher.

A man's deep, guttural voice echoed out around us, growling out three very clear words: 'What you want.'

We wondered what it meant. Was it asking, 'What do you want?'

'No, I know,' said another colleague. 'We were asking for things to be thrown, for them to use their voice, and that is what they have done. They have moved an object and have spoken, so it's saying it's what you want.'

Then another vocal surprise was captured. This noise made the hairs on the back of my neck stand up. It was a young voice, and whilst it wasn't clear what they were saying, a child's happy chatter was definitely picked up by the laptop. Had we caught the sound of a ghost child who we had heard had been seen many times in the theatre? I believe that, yes, we had.

This was an exceptional building with so many ghosts that were happy to interact with us.

Was the paranormal activity caught in the dressing room the work of the ghostly ballerina? Was the spirit of the reported hooded figure in the cellar responsible for slamming the doors? And what of the light bulb and demonic voice on the stage? Well, I definitely think that was the work of the mischievous stagehand, Charlie. Do you?

? DID YOU KNOW? ?

Water is a great conductor of spiritual energy. So the well under the stage in the theatre could in essence be adding more energy to the ghosts in the building.

Danu is believed by some to be the goddess of water wells, and is honoured in various forms of witchcraft. She is thought to be a divine source, a teacher, healer and a mother of magic. Water is one of earth's elements and is incredibly powerful. This could be why no one has been able to lay the spirits of the Lyceum Theatre to rest. Maybe it's time to seal up the well?

CRAIG Y NOS

LOCATION
WALES

GHOSTS
ADELINA PATTI

THE VICTORIAN GENTLEMAN

HOSPITAL PATIENTS

PARANORMAL ACTIVITY

DOORS OPENING AND CLOSING

NOISES OF CLOTHES RUSTLING ON THE STAIRS

VOICES HEARD

MOANING AND SIGHING

FOOTSTEPS

DARK SHADOWS

LIGHT ANOMALIES

GHOSTLY SINGING

LANE

THE HISTORY

Craig Y Nos

This is a special theatre because it has a love story attached to it. In 1842 Captain Powell built a wonderful and enormous castle but it's believed that somehow during its construction the captain and his family were cursed. By what and why, no one really knows, but it's certain that bad luck soon befell the family time and time again. Nearly all of the captain's children died of illness or accidents, then the captain himself became blind and eventually he went insane.

The castle was then sold to another family,

the Morgans, who only lived there for a couple of years until in 1878 it was bought by a world-famous opera singer, Adelina Patti. She moved into her impressive abode, renamed it Craig Y Nos, which means 'Rock of the Night', and proceeded to build a beautiful theatre inside.

For many years her friends were treated to performances of Adelina's beautiful singing in there. But Adelina was not the only famous person to perform in the theatre. The brilliant composer Gioachino Rossini visited the castle many times and performed there, and some people believe that these two musicians were in love. In fact, upon her death Adelina requested that she be buried next to Rossini in France.

In 1919, when Adelina died, the property was sold and it became a hospital for tuberculosis patients for many years.

THE HAUNTINGS

ADELINA PATTI

The main apparition that has been seen so many times in this unique theatre is that of Adelina Patti. She is often seen all around the castle but predominantly in her beloved theatre.

According to local legend, whenever anyone sings or plays the song 'Home Sweet Home' in the castle, one of Adelina's songs, her ghost materialises.

THE VICTORIAN GENTLEMAN

A very smart gentleman dressed in Victorian clothing has also been witnessed throughout the building. Many people believe this to be the spirit of Gioachino Rossini, her famous lover.

HOSPITAL PATIENTS

Along the narrow, dark corridors and staircases, figures in white long robes have also been seen and it's thought that these are the ghosts of some of the TB patients who sadly lost their lives when the castle was a sanitorium.

THE INVESTIGATION

For this investigation, back in 2004, I again invited my friend Brian Shepherd to see if he could give me more information about Adelina and her theatre, using his psychic sketches.

As we began walking the empty, dark corridors, I asked him what he could see and if there were any spirits with us, listening in to our conversation.

Brian closed his eyes and began to concentrate. The rest of the investigation team and I waited in silence, eager to find out if we were alone or not.

'There's a woman here,' Brian said, his eyes still tightly closed. 'She's very elegant, Victorian. She comes from the theatre and music; there's so much music surrounding her. But she's not alone.'

Brian paused and opened his eyes briefly.

I asked who was with her.

'It's a man, very smartly dressed, I think they're a couple. A husband? Or could be a lover?'

Was Brian picking up on the spirit of Rossini, the composer? I believed he was, and the ghost of Adelina too. I then asked Brian to draw what he could see and sure enough after a short while, Brian produced an uncanny likeness to existing portraits of the musical pair.

I then went with some of my team up onto the top floor of the castle, which was derelict and freezing cold. It was so dark that when I put my hand in front of my face, I couldn't see it. I instantly felt on edge, as did the rest of the team. There were empty rooms coming off long corridors, their doors like open black gaping chasms.

I turned around quickly, as I was sure I could hear voices behind us, as if a group of unseen people had followed us along the corridor.

'I heard that!' said the sound man. 'It sounds

like a load of people having a chat, but very low, they're murmuring.'

Then came a noise that none of us could miss. One long, loud sigh. A sound that sent chills through my body. Someone was watching us, following us and listening to what we were saying.

Meanwhile, I had sent two investigators down to the cellar, the place where Adelina's body had been embalmed and apparently where many people report seeing all manner of strange shadows and lights. Would Adelina come out to play in there?

An apparition didn't show itself, but something was apparently trying to let the two investigators know that it was present. Both men heard and caught on camera an awful dragging noise followed by a deep sighing. Unfortunately, they couldn't pinpoint exactly where they had heard the frightening sound, which was very frustrating for them.

But then one of the investigators began to panic and suddenly felt claustrophobic and incredibly anxious. His fellow investigator could tell something was wrong and so the pair left the area very quickly. What had made the investigator feel this way? Had a spirit come too close to him? Normally he was very brave, so to see him react in this manner was rather surprising. He was convinced something was with them in the cellar and he didn't like it.

I wanted to concentrate on the theatre as this was where most energy would have been expelled. All those performances, the nerves, the emotions, the singing and the applause. Energy like that, I believe, is what holds some spirits to certain buildings. And theatres are one of these places.

I positioned a large circular table in the centre of the stage and asked everyone to sit around it. Then we began to play a recording of Adelina singing. Whilst the music floated creepily around the room, I asked everyone to concentrate as I began to call out for her spirit to draw close. The famous opera singer's voice sang out 'Home Sweet Home', and the tune tumbled and echoed strangely around the inky black room. I was so sure her ghost would show itself. I called and called her name, wanting desperately for her to come and join us on the stage.

One camera operator was filming the seating area and he cried out that he'd caught some strange flashing white lights moving about in front of him. When I looked back at the footage,

I could clearly see peculiar orb-like lights moving and flashing around the auditorium. Could this have been the first manifestation of Adelina Patti's ghost? I was sure it was and so I continued talking to her, encouraging her to come onto the stage and draw closer.

Suddenly the temperature in the room dropped dramatically, so much so that the team around the table began to shake, their teeth chattering. And then we all heard a woman's long contented sigh.

I know we'd had activity like that before, but to me this was a spirit pleased at hearing her song. I just wish Adelina had taken a full curtain call.

Craig Y Nos certainly is an unusual building. I admire the fact that a talented woman bought the castle, using her own wealth, which was a rarity for women in those days. And I love the fact that she then had her own theatre built inside it. She also had her own image painted on the backdrop of the stage, where she's depicted riding a chariot pulled along by two fierce-looking horses.

She was in love with a man whom she could never truly have in life, as she herself was married. Only in death are they finally united.

DID YOU KNOW?

Certain tones, notes and frequencies can encourage paranormal activity.

During investigations I love to use a Tibetan singing bowl. This is a small copper bowl that, when the edge is run over by a small mallet, makes a high-pitched sound that seems to attract ghosts.

PAVILION THEATRE

LOCATION

CROMER, NORFOLK

THE GHOSTS ON THE PIER

MEDIEVAL FIGURES

A MAN WEARING A TALL BLACK HAT

A MAN WITH JET BLACK HAIR

LOST SAILORS

LIFEBOAT MEN

THE GHOSTS IN THE THEATRE

THE EX-EMPLOYEE

RICHARD 'DICK' CONDON

BACKSTAGE MISCHIEF-MAKERS

PARANORMAL ACTIVITY

SINGING AND HUMMING

POLTERGEIST ACTIVITY

SICKENING FEELING

THE HISTORY

Pavilion Theatre

Cromer has had a pier since 1391. Over the centuries, due to violent weather and rough seas, the pier has been demolished, replaced, demolished again and rebuilt.

In 1901 a much sturdier pier was constructed, this time from iron. The Pavilion Theatre sits proudly at the end of the pier, hanging over the North Sea's dramatic waves. Opposite the theatre sits the lifeboat station.

The theatre was constructed in 1905 and became an incredibly popular location in the early twentieth century. During World War Two the middle section of Cromer Pier was removed, and the theatre closed. When the theatre was eventually reopened, it enjoyed a brief period of entertaining the masses once more, but it wasn't long before Mother Nature made her presence felt yet again, and in 1953 the theatre and pier were battered and damaged by fierce gales. But what of its ghosts and the stories that haunt the place?

THE HAUNTINGS ON THE PIER

There have been many lives lost on and around Cromer Pier, so perhaps it's no wonder that there have been numerous reports of strange and spooky goings-on there since the 1300s!

The low, distressing cries of sailors have been heard calling out for help. Often people will rush to the end of the pier, thinking someone needs saving, only to discover that no one is there.

The ghosts of lifeboat men have also been witnessed moving quickly from the station along the pier as though setting off to save more lives.

In fact, scraggy and shadowy black apparitions of men wandering the pier from hundreds of years ago have been seen time and time again, with no logical explanation. And the fleeting image of two men, one wearing a tall black hat, the other with jet black hair, have been seen walking and gliding about the area.

Whispering voices and strange lights, black shadows, pitiful sighs and cries have all been reported on this pier.

THE HAUNTINGS IN THE THEATRE

THE EX-EMPLOYEE

The ghost of an ex-employee is said to haunt the theatre. It's believed that this man loved his job so much that he refuses to leave, even after his death.

One night some people were talking about the said gentleman, and not very favourably. Suddenly, everyone stopped speaking as the shelf at the back of the bar collapsed, taking all of its glass bottles with it. As you can imagine this caused quite a smash, and the gossip about the gentleman stopped immediately. People believe that the ex-employee was listening in and didn't like what he was hearing.

RICHARD 'DICK' CONDON

An Irish theatre impresario, named Richard 'Dick' Condon, was heavily involved with Cromer Pier. It is believed that his spirit has been seen all over the theatre. Some actors have reported seeing him on the stage, or actually standing next to them whilst they were performing. Mr Condon seems to be another ghost who simply loves still being at the theatre.

BACKSTAGE MISCHIEF-MAKERS

Backstage, there are several dressing rooms, each located off a long corridor. Staff and performers have reported on numerous occasions the feeling of being watched, the sounds of singing and shuffling of feet and knocking and tapping when there is no one else in the vicinity.

THE INVESTIGATION

I love investigating an unusual location. A haunted theatre built above the North Sea . . . well, I knew this was going to be one of those ghost hunts I would never forget.

During the early years of filming our investigations for the TV show *Most Haunted*, I was intrigued by psychics. Over the years I have invited many of them to join us in various locations around the country.

I had heard of a well-regarded American medium called Patrick Mathews, and I read one of his books. After conversations over the phone, I asked him to join us. So, on a cold, blustery winter's day in 2009, myself and the team met Patrick at the pier. Would he be able to shed any light on some of the ghostly sightings?

I wanted to begin outside, on the pier. My team turned the cameras on and I began to encourage Patrick, a softly-spoken man, to get the spirits to communicate with him.

It wasn't long before he came up with some interesting information. He told us that he could see lots of phantom ships but there was one ship in particular that was sinking, and he claimed he could hear the sailors crying out for help.

I knew this to be a phenomenon that many people had reported before, so I pushed him for more details.

He suddenly pointed over towards the land and said he could see what looked like a castle sinking into the water. The other members of the team and I were a bit confused. But our historian later told us that this had indeed happened.

Apparently, a whole town was swallowed by the sea in the 1400s.

I then suggested that we head into the theatre, as I was eager to discover who or what had been causing some of the paranormal activity inside.

As soon as we walked into the auditorium, Patrick immediately spoke out, saying he could see a woman standing in the middle of the stage. 'She's dressed in clothes from the early twentieth century, and she's saying to me politely, "This is mine," and she wants us to know it. She has a story to tell.'

According to Patrick, her ghost was beckoning us all onto the stage. And so, we all approached where her ghost was allegedly standing. It was an eerie experience.

Patrick then went on to explain a scene that the spirit of the woman was revealing to him in his mind. She was showing him someone being strangled, right there on the stage.

'Is this a scene from a play that she's showing you?' I asked.

'No, this is real, she was actually killed here,' said Patrick. Apparently the ghost was called Elizabeth.

Then Patrick told us that another spirit had joined her on the stage. 'He's an actor. George Henry is the name I'm getting. He was here when the murder took place but he's saying that he didn't do it.'

I asked when all this had happened, as it wasn't a story I was familiar with.

'Elizabeth is saying "My time",' said Patrick.

'So, that would be in the nineteen-tens?' I asked.

'The nineteen-twenties,' Patrick corrected.

I suggested that now would be a good time to go backstage to the dressing rooms. Would we connect with Elizabeth there? I hoped so. I wanted more information.

The backstage area had a strange, unpleasant atmosphere and as soon as my feet crossed the threshold I knew that we were not alone. Someone was watching us.

As there were quite a few of us, some were positioned in a dressing room, and others in the corridor, but as soon as we began to talk about Elizabeth, we heard a strange and spine-chilling humming noise.

We all asked each other the usual and important question: 'Was that you?' so that we could eliminate any noises that we might have made ourselves. There are numerous times when investigators have screamed, thinking a demonic growl has been experienced, when in fact it's just been a rumbly tummy from another member of the team digesting a late-night burger. (The diet of a ghost hunter isn't really very healthy at all.)

After we had all agreed that none of us had hummed, I called out again. This time, I hummed out the tune of the national anthem, hoping to get the spirit to copy me.

Suddenly, a long, loud note was hummed out for us all to hear once more. I hummed out again, this time another simple tune. There! A few more ghostly notes came back for us to hear. We managed to capture the sound on our recording equipment and I was thrilled about it.

I called out several more times but nothing else came back and so I decided to return to the stage area and take Patrick and the rest of the team with me.

As we all stood on that empty stage, Patrick began to talk with the spirit of George Henry again. The ghost was explaining to him that the murder had occurred on the stage, and the audience had actually believed it was part of the play. He relayed to Patrick that the 'rumours were correct'. George Henry continued to talk through Patrick, saying that he wanted to put the mystery to rest and that the death of the woman was an accident. Apparently, Elizabeth was very frustrated at not becoming a star. The spirit of Elizabeth then began to speak to Patrick. She told him that she was in a scene where she was to be strangled, but the other actor went too far and killed her. But because she was an unknown actor, they covered it up, and the murder was never reported.

After we had all been given this riveting information, we didn't know what to think. I decided to push on and instructed all the lights in the theatre be turned off.

I'm often asked, 'Why don't you investigate in the daytime?' Good question. This is something I love doing and we have managed to capture some amazing paranormal phenomena in the daylight, but it's adrenalin that makes energy. In turn, the spirits, ghosts and entities feed off our nervous energy and use it to make more things happen. So, walking around a creepy theatre in the pitch dark can really help to pump that fear factor up, hence more fuel for the spooks.

A group of three very brave ghost hunters shakily made their way to the backstage areas. Would the ghost of Elizabeth come out and sing to them one more time? Or perhaps the impresario might make an entrance. I hoped that they would capture something on camera for us all to see.

They began in a dressing room and started by calling out to the ghosts of Elizabeth and George.

Within seconds of them asking for the spirits to step forward, knocking and tapping began to thump from the ceiling and walls. Then, as if on cue, the singing and humming began. It was extraordinary: clear, haunting and very scary. And it was all caught on our cameras.

We then went back to the stage area; I was drawn to it. This could have been the scene of a real murder. How sad, yet fascinating.

The night continued into the early hours of the morning, with two investigators going under the stage, which resulted in objects being thrown at them from a very aggressive poltergeist and one investigator being violently sick.

We also conducted a Ouija board session on the pier and contacted Elizabeth once more, who then told us her father had been killed by falling off the pier. His name was David but she referred to him as 'Pop'. The end of the Ouija session culminated with the board lifting up into the air several times and the glass whizzing off the table at a furious speed. After that, all went quiet. We had come to the end of our investigation and what an adventure we had all had! There are so many questions that need answering. I seriously need to go back. Want to come with me?

THE OLDHAM COLISEUM

THE GHOSTS
HAROLD NORMAN

DARK ENTITIES

CARL PAULSEN

PARANORMAL ACTIVITY
OBJECTS MAKING NOISES

FURNITURE MOVING

STATIC DARK FIGURES THAT ROCK FROM SIDE TO SIDE

LOCATION
MANCHESTER

THE HISTORY

Oldham Coliseum

The land on which this theatre sits today was once used for mining. It was a relatively poor area but by the late 1800s a building was constructed and welcomed locals inside to watch a circus perform.

Buffalo Bill's *Wild West Show* came to perform here as did Fred Karno's circus. Lions, tigers, bears, elephants and horses all entertained the audiences of the day, and let's not forget the world-famous comics Stan Laurel and Charlie Chaplin, who trod the boards here too. Is there anywhere these two didn't perform in the UK? Famous film stars such as Ralph Fiennes and Minnie Driver also began their illustrious careers in this building.

During the 1930s the building briefly became a cinema but it closed after a decline in the number of movie-goers, and the theatre was opened. The Coliseum was affectionately known as 'the people's theatre'. Due to a withdrawal of funding, it sadly closed its doors for the last time on 31st March 2023. I'll bet the ghosts still play there though.

THE HAUNTINGS

HAROLD NORMAN

The ghost of actor Harold Norman has apparently been seen countless times sitting in the circle area watching the stage. In 1947, he was tragically stabbed during a performance whilst playing the part of Macbeth. He managed to crawl off to the wings where he was attended to by a first aider but sadly passed away from blood poisoning some weeks later.

DARK ENTITIES

Under the stage, there seems to lurk a dark, menacing shadow of a spirit. No one has seen its features, but the staff hate going down there for fear of seeing the malevolent entity. It's said to stand in one spot and sway from side to side.

A five-foot black shadow of a ghost has also been witnessed walking from the circle area and through a wall which leads straight into the wardrobe department.

CARL PAULSEN

The apparition of a tall woman dressed in a black Victorian dress has also appeared in the wardrobe department area. Many people believe this to be the spirit of Carl Paulsen. He worked at the theatre for many years as director of productions. He was also an actor and, on several occasions, played women on stage.

THE INVESTIGATION

I was so excited to be able to spend the night in one of Manchester's beloved theatres. This place has so many happy memories for so many Mancunians, my dad being one of them. So, in 2004 we entered the doors of this wonderful theatre.

On hearing that not one, but two ghosts resided in the wardrobe department, I wanted to get up there straight away to have a look about.

The lights were all off as usual and I hoped a ghostly manifestation was going to show itself. I began walking with my fellow ghost hunters along the narrow dark passageway, towards the wardrobe department.

As we walked slowly along, I was suddenly aware of a smell. It was a burning smell, not a quick whiff, but a powerful, strong smell, as if something were on fire. I asked my colleagues and they too said they could smell it. Was there a fire in the building? I radioed to the rest of the team who were in different parts of the theatre, and they replied that they couldn't smell anything and that there was no need for alarm.

I wasn't satisfied, and so I began to search each room, checking in case there was indeed a fire, but thank goodness I found nothing untoward. How extraordinary! Suddenly the smell disappeared as quickly as it had come.

I did wonder if we had experienced some kind of Stone Tape Theory effect. This is where some people believe, me included, that the stones of a building act as a video tape recorder, sucking into its walls the images, sounds and smells of many of its past inhabitants. Only when the right temperature, air pressure and weather conditions are all aligned can the image be transmitted back into the location.

The most famous case of this is said to have occurred in the cellar of the Treasurer's House in York. This incredible sighting was of fifteen Roman soldiers marching through the basement, complete with neighing horses. The terrified onlooker recounted that all the soldiers were only visible from the knees up. Afterwards, research archaeologists discovered that the house was now on top of what used to be a very busy Roman road. But the extraordinary feature was that the road used to be eighteen inches below the new floor level. So that's why the soldiers' feet were not visible. These images were just that, not ghosts at all but a wonderful case of the Stone Tape Theory in action.

As the land that the Oldham Coliseum theatre was built on had been used for mining, had we smelled some of the coal mining techniques used all that time ago? I suspect so.

Inside the wardrobe room, mannequins and tailors' dummies stood motionless around us. I scanned my night-vison camera about the room, calling out as I did. I knew we were being watched. Whoever it was that was with us wasn't happy. My tummy flip-flopped, and I wanted to go. I wasn't alone in that feeling, as two other team members also felt the same. We decided to leave and headed back along the passageway, down the stairs and under the stage.

This was the place where the staff hated coming alone and I'm not at all surprised. What a hideous place this was. Pitch-black and claustrophobic. A corridor leading off to a larger room that housed some sort of large machinery, and a huge monster of an old boiler sat like an ancient, rusty sentinel, waiting to growl into action at any moment.

I shuffled into the black room and huddled up closer to my two companions. I called out, hoping to get a reaction from the spirit that had been seen down there many times. I squeezed my eyes shut tight, as I really didn't fancy seeing a tall dark shadow, swaying to and fro in front of me. I drew in a long deep breath and gave myself a mental telling off: *Pull yourself together, woman, you're supposed to be a paranormal investigator! Now open your eyes and call out to the spirits!* I called out quietly, 'Can you give me a sign to let me know that you can see and hear us?'

As soon as the last word tumbled out of my quivering mouth, a hideous loud noise smashed into my torso. It rumbled and growled around the room, instantly making my knees buckle in abject terror.

The large piece of machinery, which I later found out was a generator, had kicked mysteriously into life, nearly taking my last breath with it. I had screamed so loudly, I'd actually damaged my throat.
It took a while after
this incident for
it to feel less
rough and
scratched.

I was told by the manager of the theatre that the generator shouldn't have gone off, it was highly unusual and wasn't capable of being activated in the early hours of the morning by itself. I couldn't help but think of how perfectly timed it was. The noise had occurred directly after I had asked for something to happen. Was a ghost responsible for starting the generator? I'd like to think it was.

One investigator decided to sit quietly in the circle area of the theatre and try to see if they could get a message from the ghost of Harold Norman.

He sat patiently and kept calling out Harold's name, and his tolerance paid off, as on camera you can clearly hear a seat being brought down into the sitting position. The investigator didn't panic, he just simply said, 'Thank you, Harold.'

Two other investigators wanted to see if they could get a similar result and so tried the circle area too. Would the ghost of Harold come and sit next to them? Or even better, show himself?

The two investigators knew how Harold had died and so decided to call using the cursed Shakespearean play name of *Macbeth*. As soon as this word was uttered, another seat clattered down into place. *Bang!*

When I watched the footage back, there were shots of the same seat taken only moments before, by the same two investigators. The seat was up and so we now knew that something, possibly Harold, had felt comfortable enough to join the investigators.

This phenomenon has happened many times to me in various theatres and I love it when we manage to capture the sound. However, we've never managed to film a seat moving from the up position to the down in one movement.

So, back to the two investigators in the circle.

At the same time as the seat fell into place, they both began to feel cold. An icy spot could be felt right between them and one of the investigators began to shudder with the sudden and extreme drop in temperature.

They called out again to Harold and asked for another sign. They weren't disappointed. One after the other, three beautiful bright light anomalies or orbs floated slowly across the camera screen. Dust, or the first manifestation of Harold? I like to think it was Harold, as do my two colleagues.

I wonder if since our investigation the paranormal activity has increased or dissipated. Are the spirits of Harold, Carl and the dark ones still there? I bet the staff still hate going under the stage nevertheless.

DID YOU KNOW?

Sometimes you can capture an orb or light anomaly on film. When zoomed into or enlarged, you might see a ghostly face in the centre.

I was very lucky as I managed to capture a bright blue orb on an old phone camera. When I blew the photograph up on my laptop I was astounded and thrilled to see my father's face in the orb. The picture was of me celebrating my fortieth birthday and there, as plain as anything to me, was my dad, who had passed away some years earlier, smiling down on me.

So, maybe have a look through some old family photographs and look out for a circular light. Take a magnifying glass or, if you can, zoom in on your computer or phone. You never know, you could have discovered something paranormal.

THE GAUMONT CINEMA

THE GHOSTS

AN EVIL ENTITY

THE HANGED MAN

A SINISTER, DARK FIGURE

STONE TAPE THEORY
APPARITIONS

LOCATION

LIVERPOOL,
MERSEYSIDE

PARANORMAL ACTIVITY

POLTERGEIST ACTIVITY

COLD SPOTS

DARK MALEVOLENT SHADOWS

UNEXPLAINED GUSTS OF WINDS

DOORS OPENING AND
SLAMMING SHUT

UNEXPLAINED MOVEMENT OF
OBJECTS

BEING TOUCHED

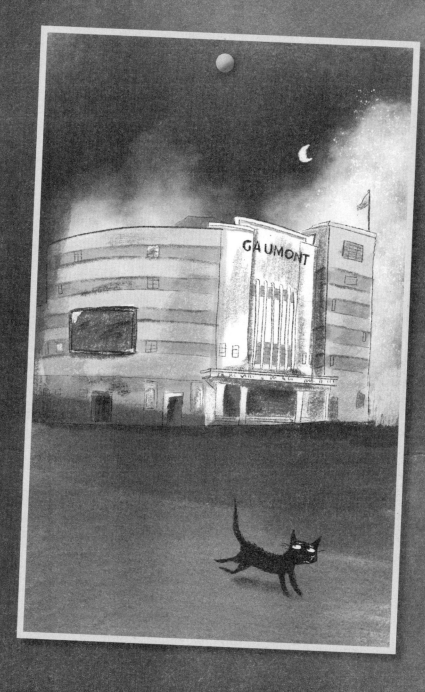

THE HISTORY

The Gaumont

The Gaumont cinema is an Art Deco building that's situated on Dingle Lane in Toxteth, Liverpool. This wonderful place sits on top of what once was the old Dingle Picturedrome. The structure we see today was designed by W. E. Trent, and was opened to the public in 1937.

It proved to be an incredibly popular place for the locals during World War Two. Thousands of Liverpudlians flocked to watch the current world news and, of course, lose themselves in the latest movie. They could immerse themselves in a world of sparkle and make-believe and forget about the world outside. This was a place where you could ignore your troubles, relax, and join the sophisticated movie stars up there on the big silver screen.

In 1966 the Gaumont shut up shop as a cinema and reopened as a bingo hall the following year. Now the building stands empty and derelict. A sad sight to see, but as soon as I stepped inside, I knew we were in for an entertaining night.

THE HAUNTINGS

AN EVIL ENTITY

An evil entity is alleged to reside in the basement. Something likes to open the doors and slam them shut. People report being touched by unseen hands.

Many people believe that the entity lurking deep below the ground casts a dark shadow over the entire building. This menacing spirit is said to have a hold on all the other spirits that dwell inside the location. When this dark, sinister ghost does reveal itself it's supposed to appear in a terrifying form.

THE HANGED MAN

Not much is known about this ghost but apparently some years ago a gentleman took his own life on stage. He hanged himself in the centre of the stage, and since his demise his spirit is said to become very angry if anyone steps into the space where he took his last breath.

A SINISTER, DARK FIGURE

Up in the attic is where another malevolent creature is said to lurk. It waits and hides in the dark corners and recesses of the highest part of the theatre.

Cold spots race past any unfortunate soul who happens to be up there, followed by an unusual loud howling wind that rushes past, with no logical explanation.

STONE TAPE THEORY APPARITIONS

Witnesses have often reported seeing a row of ghosts sitting silently staring up at where the screen of the cinema used to be.

My belief is that this is another example of Stone Tape Theory and that the building has absorbed energies and memories from the past. When the right temperature, air pressure and atmosphere is reached, that memory or scene is played out for us to see years after the original act occurred.

THE INVESTIGATION

It was such a shame to see that a beautiful building which had brought joy to so many people had fallen into disrepair. It was 2009 and I was saddened as I crept around, and I could feel an air of loneliness and despair. There was more than one spirit here, that much I could tell, and they were not at all happy.

We began this investigation at the lowest point of the building and worked our way up to the top, the dreaded attic.

In the basement, the atmosphere was incredibly tense, and my team of investigators were nervous. You could feel static energy in the air, yet where that energy was coming from, we didn't know. But we could tell it wasn't natural. It was like we were surrounded, hemmed in by lots of spirits. We stayed close together and I began to call out loudly, trying not to show any fear.

'Come on, come and say hello. Do something to let us know that you're here with us. I know you're here. I can feel your presence.'

Well, I and the rest of the team then got the fright of our lives as something smashed with extreme force right in the middle of the group. Instantly all the torches went on and lit up the derelict, dusty room.

Broken glass lay scattered all around our feet, and then one of the investigators shouted out, 'Listen!'

We all stood still and heard what can only be described as something being dragged along the floor. The noise was coming from behind a boiler. One investigator went round to look but reported that nothing was there. It was strange but not unusual, because this is quite a common noise associated with the paranormal and my least favourite sound.

I suspected we had been joined by something malevolent, and we needed to be careful, but I was fascinated. Who was this spirit, and why did it feel so angry and negative?

We turned our torches off again and stood silently, waiting for something else to happen. We didn't have long to wait. Suddenly another smash echoed throughout the room.

Instantly we lit the room again and found a light bulb on the floor. But the strange thing was, it wasn't broken. So, what had smashed? We couldn't find any glass or any logical explanation as to what had made the sound.

We put the unbroken light bulb on a shelf and took a photo of it just so we had a record of where we had placed it and at what time. We also made sure that no one could enter that area again, so if the light bulb moved, we knew it wasn't one of us who had interfered with it.

We walked through the basement and into another smaller room and suddenly one of the investigators yelped in shock that something had hit his foot.

He bent down and picked up something small and circular. An old coin.

The torches went back on again and we all gathered round to look at an old three pence piece dated from 1964.

This wasn't the first time we had been hit with coins from a different era and I hoped not the last.

It was now time to go to the stage area. I wanted to see if we could contact the unfortunate gentleman who had hanged himself on the stage. I really hoped to get some answers about who he was. Maybe a Ouija board session on the stage directly underneath where he had met his end would get a response from his ghost.

So, six of us were sitting there and all keen to get going. The auditorium was huge, and the stage was raised three metres above the floor. From where we were sitting there was a big drop down to the ground. We sat in total darkness and waited. I began to whisper out into the dark void.

'Is there anybody with us?'

As if in answer, an enormous rush of wind whistled past. It was an unnerving noise and there was no obvious reason as to why it had happened. Was that the spirits talking to us?

I called out again, this time slower and with more confidence, and sure enough, the big wooden table that we were sitting around began to rock. At first they were slight movements but then they became much stronger. Back and forth the heavy table heaved. The energy was incredible. We soon realised that the table was walking across the stage by itself. We stood up and went with it, our fingers hardly touching the wooden top. A couple of the team walked away, scared at this incredible activity.

'If you don't want us on your stage, then push the table over the edge,' I was shouting now, really determined to get a good reaction. 'If this is the man who killed himself, here on this stage, then push the table harder, go on,' I urged.

The table banged and bounced about, objects began to rain down from above, hitting us in the back as we walked with the table closer and closer to the edge of the stage and then, off it went crashing down to the ground, smashing into pieces at the bottom.

All went quiet, no one spoke, and the activity died too. The light bulb we had put away and photographed hadn't moved.

All that remained was a stillness, a menacing silence. The whole building felt vile. I knew if we stayed, something truly awful would happen. I sensed that this spirit meant real harm and I wasn't about to let one of my crew members get injured.

We had our answer. The man who haunted the stage was telling us to get out and we didn't need telling twice.

DID YOU KNOW?

Old pennies have been amongst the many items that seemingly appear from nowhere in a haunted location. This paranormal activity is more commonly known as an 'apport'. This is when small objects suddenly drop or are thrown into a room at an unsuspecting guest.

This has happened to me and my team many times and I now have a fine collection of really old pennies, dating back as far as the 1600s.

The first time the Most Haunted team encountered an apport of old pennies was in a creepy abandoned farmhouse. While we were in the attic, a shower of old coins pelted us from the ceiling. There were possibly fifty of them. What was even stranger is that the pennies all landed heads up. I discovered that this is apparently a good sign; it is meant as a gift from the spirit world. I call them pennies from heaven and have made a few into badges that I wear on my coat with pride.